1

# Wartime Childhood

*Audrey Lanceman*

Published by David Brown
2 West Street Farm Cottages
Maynards Green
Heathfield
Sussex  TN21 0DG


ISBN 0 9514641 1 6

*Class photograph, Ring Cross Primary School, Islington 1939*
*Audrey Lanceman is in the back row at the centre of the*
*photograph*

*This book is dedicated to
my old playmate Iris*

# Acknowledgements

The cover photograph is reproduced by kind permission of Bernard Delves. The ownership of other illustrations in the book is as follows:
Ilustrations on pages 11, 19, 23, 24, 25 and 29 drawn by Audrey Lanceman during the time she was evacuated to Balsham.
Photographs on pages 6 and 7: David Brown taken during 2005
Photographs on pages iii and 17: Audrey Lanceman.
Photographs on pages 2 and 32 courtesy of the London Borough of Islington – Library and Cultural Services
Photograph on page 13 of unknown provenance, reproduced on a Balsham calendar in recent years.

# *Preface*

I have thought so often about the war years and felt I must write about it one day.

I never seemed to have the time until a knee operation prevented me from standing at the easel.

I have such clear memories of the village of Balsham and thinking back, of how everyone's lives were affected and changed; I thought it worth recording mine.

I would like this generation to know how it felt when, with no choice or control, one found oneself swept along by events into an uncertain future.

Audrey Lanceman
September 2005

### ৺৪ *Chapter 1* ৪৵

The summer of 1939 was hot and sultry. My sister and I could not sleep and we were aware of our parents and neighbours standing outside in the street, discussing the impending war.

My father had a tailor's shop in the Holloway Road, we lived upstairs. There was an air of foreboding in the atmosphere. One evening we all had to go to Islington library to be fitted with gas masks. I found this rather frightening; I was eight at the time. At school, my brother David recalls that we had rehearsals, filing through the streets to the tube station. I don't remember that, but I do remember being very excited when we were told to be at school very early in the morning as we were going to the country for about two weeks until the war clouds blew over. After all the suspense we were finally to leave London on the morning of 1 September 1939.

From the school we marched in file to Holloway Road tube station. A group of mothers had gathered outside our shop as we passed by. My sister and I were in high spirits, with no notion of the seriousness of what was happening to all these children making their grand exit from London.

*I passed this warehouse each day on my way to school in Eden Grove. It was just a large wall to me. It was just behind my house on Holloway Road and was hit after I had been evacuated.*

But as we passed the shop, waving, I saw tears running down my mother's bravely smiling face.

For a brief moment my high spirits were dampened but soon all was forgotten as, from the underground, we poured into King's Cross station. The station was swarming with evacuees, labels round their necks, gas masks on their backs, clutching carrier bags or small bundles with minimum necessities.

We sat in the same carriage as our two teachers. They had no more idea of where we were going than we had but as the guard passed along the corridor Miss Lillie called to

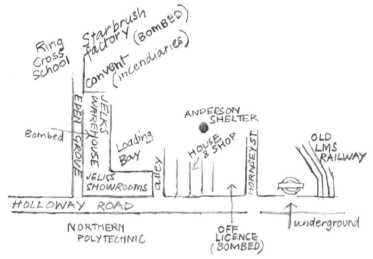

him and asked for the train's destination. "Cambridge," whispered the guard. Miss Lillie and Miss Pearce looked pleased and we felt pleased too.

But as we left the station on that fateful morning little did we know that we would never return to Islington, that chapter of our lives was closed.

———————◆———————

Arriving at Cambridge station we were guided into a makeshift area where we were given a drink and a carrier of emergency supplies. Biscuits and two tins of corned beef, I seem to remember, and a stamped postcard to be sent to our parents. Next we were herded into waiting buses. Ours was a double-decker and we climbed on top.

The bus headed down country lanes with overhanging branches striking against the windows, all adding to the air of excitement and adventure. It was a ten-mile journey to the village of Balsham, where our bus emptied. The single-decker behind with the rest of our school was waved on and headed for the next village of West Wratting.

We were ushered into the village schoolhouse to await our fate. But no sooner had we sat down at the desks than a group of village women entered the room and started picking out the evacuees they wanted, instead of waiting for the billeting officer to allocate places. It was like an animal auction, and as we didn't like the look of these women Jean and I hid under the desk. When we surfaced the room was half empty and the women had gone. We had to stick together; my brother had already been whisked off. Our names were called out and we set off with a young billeting officer in an old Austin Seven.

We drove back to the edge of the village, where a row of council houses stood back from the Cambridge road. There was a little stream and a bridge to cross to the house entrance. Mrs Beeton stood waiting to greet us. Unfortunately she was given a third evacuee, which was more than she asked for, and Rose was no particular friend of ours. I felt dismayed when I saw the bed we were all to share, as, being the smallest, I knew I would be the one to be squashed in the middle. I did not dwell on such matters then as I could not wait to be out exploring and I am sure

Mrs Beeton was equally keen on us going out. After a corned beef sandwich and a tomato from the garden, we were off. Rose fortunately found that her friend was billeted next door so we were not encumbered with her presence.

Not far from the house, in a hollow of the Hildersham road, was a haystack in the meadow and that is where we headed. Before long others joined us and our loud whoops of delight attracted yet more evacuees as we slid and tumbled down the haystack. It must have belonged to a kind farmer as no one came to tell us to stop. Soon we found our brother; he came down the lane with five other boys, pockets stuffed with apples.

The six boys had been billeted with Mr Gedney, the village grocer, and they had already raided his orchard. Apart from David they were pretty rough boys, which must have overwhelmed the rather elderly grocer. Soon the other boys were re-billeted and only David remained with Mr Gedney. He helped him with deliveries and was very willing to please as he got very attached to the family and stayed on in the one billet for the whole of the period, whereas Jean and I had three different billets.

Two days later, on 3 September, war was declared. We had no wireless so we listened to Chamberlain's speech from the door of our neighbour. It was a beautiful peaceful morning and I suppose we did not realise the implications of those words drifting out across the garden.

*The village school, now a private residence*

The Beetons had a spaniel named Terry who followed us nearly everywhere. We were sent out to pick blackberries but came across sloes and I thought they were grapes. We decided that Auntie Min (as we now called her) would prefer those and took her back a basketful. But we soon began to learn country lore and the names of wild flowers.

Our schooling, when it began, was highly inadequate. The village school was left for the village children. The boys took over the old schoolhouse. The rest of us, from infants to twelve-year-olds, were massed together in the Village Institute. A section was screened off for the infants and the rest of us, of various ages, were put into the

*The Village Institute as it is today*

remaining space with makeshift desks, which had to be removed whenever the hall was needed. At the far end was a stage. For heating there was an old coke stove, which gave out more smoke than heat.

The stage was very useful for putting on plays. My sister was very happy with this, performing whenever she could or doing cartwheels when the teacher wasn't looking. Because of the variety of ages our lessons consisted mainly of country dancing, nature walks, writing essays, sewing and drawing; the two former subjects as a means of keeping warm in the winter. When the temperature dropped we went out for a brisk walk and learned the names of plants and trees. Because of my aptitude for drawing I was often left alone to draw instead of doing other things.

The toilet facilities were very primitive, a dirt closet out at the back of the Village Institute. But equally, neither did most cottages have modern facilities. Our billet was a council house but there was no electricity or bathroom. When it came to bath day Mrs Beeton would light the copper in the corner of the kitchen and fill it with water and we would climb in. Our washing water came from the rainwater butt outside. That first winter of 1939/40 was very bitter. The butt froze and we had to break the ice to get water: we thought this was fun. I remember there was a pump outside, shared between the cottages for drinking water, and this is where the village gossips would gather and watch us pass, muttering, "There goes them evacuees".

Snow fell heavily and stayed hard and crisp for weeks, the horse-drawn snowplough made a path through, but even Jean and I didn't care to stay outside for long. Christmas was approaching and Auntie Min set us to work making decorations. We had collected every little bit of silver paper we could find from sweet wrappers etc, which we then carefully wrapped round little ears of barley. The result was extremely pretty and, since we had never had Christmas decorations before, they were a delight, sparkling and shimmering on their stalks.

Our parents came down and visited us for Christmas, staying at the nearby pub. My father was in top form, joking and making everyone laugh. On Boxing Day the men went off coursing across the fields, mainly in pursuit of rabbits and hares. My father joined in, little knowing what he was letting himself in for. At dusk he returned in a state of collapse, much to everyone's amusement.

We relied on rabbit and pigeon to supplement our meagre rations. I have never wanted to eat pigeon since. Hare pie was a rare treat or, as Mr Beeton called it, "air pie". Our vegetables were grown in the garden.

After the joys of summer wandering along the Roman road with the dog and admiring the hedgerows full of wild roses, flowers and berries, we experienced the new delights of winter. Mr and Mrs Beeton introduced us to tobogganing. We all trudged down the Cambridge road to Devil's Dyke, a delightful place for sledging. And later, when spring showed its early face, the banks were full of paigles, violets and primroses. Each season brought new wonders; the melting snow produced babbling brooks, the water so clear and sparkling. We paddled in the icy water. It was safe to wander everywhere; there was only an occasional car and sometimes an army convoy.

In spring Mrs Beeton decided to get a nanny goat for our milk. We loved the young nanny. Before school we would take her to the top of the Hildersham road and peg her to the roadside where there was an abundance of grasses and wild flowers. Then at noon, when we returned from school for dinner, we would collect Snowy. She was always excited to see us approaching, she would gallop down the road with us, making a terrible din and tossing her heels in the air.

We saw very little of David and never gave him much thought, we were all too busy with our lives. It was usually after an air raid that we saw him. Mr Gedney was one of about four people in the village who had a telephone, the others being the post office, the manor house and perhaps the squire's house. When an air raid was expected the warning was sent through to Mr Gedney; he immediately mounted his bicycle and rode through the village blowing his whistle. For the "all clear" a large handbell was used and David was allowed to ride round the village ringing his bell and shouting "all clear". It was then that Jean and I rushed out to see him. How he loved that job. He also did most of the grocery deliveries when he came home from school.

Regarding the air raids, we had quite a few in those early days as we were not far from the East Anglian airfields. Quite frequently there were dogfights above and the occasional bomb was dropped not too far away when German bombers got rid of their loads before returning to the coast. Once a bomber was brought down a mile away and we children set off to find souvenirs from the burnt-out wreck. Mr Beeton had built an Anderson shelter in the garden and when there was a night raid we all got out of bed and trooped down, except for Mr Beeton who

*'When the Air-Raid Warning Goes'*
drawn by Audrey Lanceman

preferred to stand outside and watch the night sky for action. He had a reserved occupation, bricklaying, and every morning early, he and his brother Eric were driven to Cambridge for the building of shelters and defences.

Eric lived with his mother in a really old thatched cottage. It was quite primitive and absolutely delightful. The uneven floors were covered in rag rugs; the cottage was dark but lit by oil lamps. Outside was an old fashioned garden with a well for drinking water. The garden was stocked with lupins, sweet William, night-scented stock and roses, plus the usual vegetable patch. But what we loved most was a particular apple tree. It produced the sweetest crispest apples I had ever tasted, and so rare we never ever came across such an apple since, that tasted as good as Granny Beeton's apple.

On Saturday evenings we would all visit the cottage and make our own entertainment. Eric was musical, he played the piano but what he did also, which hypnotised Jean and me, was sit in the corner and play the musical saw. How I loved sitting there in the lamplight listening. Vera, a friend of Eric's, who worked as a maid at the manor house, would join us; her husband was away fighting in France, as was Mrs Beeton's brother.

One weekend Mr and Mrs Beeton wanted to go away to visit her sister but she couldn't leave us two girls alone. Vera asked permission of the lady of the manor, Lady Scott Miller, if we could stay two nights at the manor house in one of the many vacant rooms if Vera looked after us and kept us out of the way. It is an interesting thought that she took no evacuees even though just about every house in the village was obliged to squeeze in one or two. There were also refugees from Czechoslovakia, sad lost people who taught us some Czech national dances.

Going through the big iron gates of the manor house filled us with awe. Vera led us to our bedrooms along a long corridor. We were given a room each; I had a starched frilled pillowcase that stuck in my neck, keeping me awake.

*The Manor House*

We hadn't asked about the bathroom so found ourselves going down the long corridor opening doors and peering in until we found it.

The grounds were very well kept and orderly, there was a small lake with a cherry tree on an island. Grape hyacinths and daffodils were growing along the borders. But we dare not run about and make a noise, as we felt watched by the old gardener or Lady Scott Miller at her window.

On Saturday morning I was summoned to her office. I stood before her desk while she wrote out something and handed me some money. "I want you to go to the post office and get my car battery refilled," she said, and then she presented me with a battery, which I carefully held out two hands to receive, and I set out on my important mission.

I had to take the path through the churchyard and to my dismay I saw the familiar bicycles of Ted Plume and Doug Twitchett had been purposefully left across the entrance, blocking my way. I was in dread of dropping the battery so I kicked the bicycles with my foot, stepped over them and marched on. From the corner of my eye I could see two heads bobbing up from the ditch. These two boys had taken a fancy to Jean and me and followed us everywhere. Often, believing we were alone, walking and singing away, we would suddenly become aware of a face peering through a hedge. We got very exasperated with their game. Playing around haystacks we would unexpectedly come across their bicycles and know that they had been listening to our private chatter. They never attempted to speak to us, just pretended to be invisible. Not everyone was fascinated with us, especially when I got German measles and the village gossips complained that we had brought diseases with us from London. Though I slept in the same bed as my sister she never caught German measles, and I'm glad to say neither did Auntie Min. I was kept to my room and soon recovered.

At the Village Institute where we went to school there were various social events. The school put on concerts and the nativity play at Christmas. The events were not only to entertain the village but also to raise funds for the war effort. Lady Scott Miller arranged a dance and invited smart friends from London. I was very taken with their elegant dance dresses. There was a smattering of officers and airmen amongst the locals, and a band was provided.

At the concerts we did country dancing and Jean usually did a solo tap dance with acrobatics. The school sang patriotic songs, including a song praising Uncle Joe (Stalin) who was our ally and who, at the time, was held in high esteem.

London had been free of air raids at the beginning of the war, which lulled some of the mothers into a false sense of security. We were near airfields, so I remember well one mother, amongst several, coming down and taking her twin daughters back to London against all advice. She missed them and wanted them at home, others went back because they were unhappy in their billets. Not everyone was as fortunate as us.

Then suddenly the blitz started and we heard later that the twins were killed. We worried about our parents; they managed to visit us on a Sunday every four or five weeks when they had saved some rationed petrol. We never knew for sure whether they would make it. When they were due we would wander down the Linton road in anticipation, scanning the horizon for the sight of an old Ford. Only occasionally did we wait and wait in vain, and then wander back disappointed.

Uncle Ron, so called, the Reverend Francis from Holloway, wrote us jolly letters about his hair-raising escapes from the bombs in Holloway and we wrote back about our life in the village. His vicarage must have been hit for he was transferred to a new post in Peckham. Eden Grove suffered quite a bit of damage for our school was blitzed and I imagined my drawings, that I had last seen pinned to the classroom walls, flapping around in the breeze. Opposite the school was a factory called The Star Brush Company where all kinds of brushes were made. That got a direct hit. Two of our classmates lived next door; they had not taken part in the evacuation and unfortunately were both killed.

As summer approached we were suddenly told that we would have to be re-billeted. Mrs Beeton was expecting a baby and our room would be needed for the new infant.

We knew the village was full and viewed the prospect with trepidation. Then came news that our two teachers, Miss Lillie and Miss Pearce, would be willing to take us into their cottage. The old thatched cottage they lived in really belonged to a doctor in Cambridge, it was called Chapels-close and was near the church. It had a long front garden and a fully stocked orchard at the rear. There was a profusion of flowers at the front and an area dug out to grow vegetables. Miss Pearce was retired so she did all the gardening and cooking. Our meals were mainly garden vegetables with a sprinkling of cheese on top. We loved it and never got tired of it. I do not remember having any meat. I was quite happy to forego pigeon pie.

The cottage was very low beamed and Jean would do a

*Chapels-close, now known as April Cottage*

handstand and wedge her feet on a beam. The stairs from the living room led straight into our bedroom, then a step and a door led to Miss Lillie's room and Miss Pearce's room was beyond that, with a staircase leading down to the kitchen and bathroom. For the first time in our lives we had a bathroom and indoor toilet.

We were obliged to drink a lot, Miss Pearce having decided we were not taking enough fluids; she therefore produced bottles of homemade lemonade, which we didn't like at all. It had a clouded appearance and we had to take a glass each up to bed with us, where we devised various ways to get it down, blowing tunes into it and then taking a gulp, for example, and then guessing which tune each of us made.

When we were sent to bed we would sometimes throw each other's pyjamas down the stairs, which obliged us to creep down into the room where our teachers were quietly reading and surreptitiously retrieve them. We also devised a way of making our precious sweet ration last a bit longer by each hiding the other's portion so that we were not tempted by the accessibility of it to gobble it up too soon. It didn't really work as we couldn't resist hunting for it, also Miss Pearce would find it in the most unlikely places when she cleaned our room. Returning from school our sweets would be placed pointedly on the bed.

We were always on our best behaviour as we were a little afraid of Miss Lillie. She suffered from severe headaches and didn't want us around all the time, especially after a day at school. We were regularly sent out with a picnic tea after school and lingered out as long as possible. We discovered secret places and found a favourite tree trunk in a meadow where we would spread out our tea.

Miss Lillie worried about our lack of schooling and tried to give us a little homework but we were getting further and further behind. We did read a lot though and we certainly learned the names of the wild flowers, of

THE COTTAGE

*'The Cottage'*
*drawn by Audrey Lanceman*

which there were many. We never tired of finding new flowers with each season, discovering our first glimpses of periwinkles and violets in the woods. In Islington we only found dandelions.

Miss Pearce allowed us to bring one friend home for tea once a fortnight. This was quite a sought-after treat, but a Tuesday came around and we had forgotten to ask anyone. When we walked into the kitchen and saw the special cake and tea arranged we felt deeply ashamed.

One afternoon a week there was a schools programme on the wireless and Miss Lillie allowed the girls to come to the cottage and sit on the floor around the fire to listen. She was able to relax in her comfortable armchair. We were allowed to sew or knit. In those days there was no question of food or drink, we were very happy to be in the cottage instead of the cold village hall.

At school we made use of the stage quite a lot and on one occasion we were acting out religious scenes from the Bible. This was how Jean discovered her talent for comedy. She was cast as Peter the Fisherman, and somehow she had obtained a pair of lady's navy bloomers. When she walked onto the stage with her fishing rod, hat and bloomers, everyone burst into laughter. She looked surprised, hesitated, and then decided to play it for laughs. I looked at Miss Lillie's face, she was trying to look severe but she couldn't restrain her laughter.

The war still seemed far away but one night, as we sat up in bed blowing bubbles into our lemonade, the eerie sound of a bomb whistling through the air stopped us and, as we looked at each other and as the sound got louder and nearer, we slammed our drinks on the bedside table and threw the sheets over our heads. There was a loud explosion but it didn't come through the roof, as we feared, it landed in a field half a mile away. Then we heard the sound of Mr Gedney's whistle.

Christmas came and went and then we had heavy snow falls.

## ⚜ *Chapter 2* ⚜

**I**n the middle of January, when it was bleak, the days short and dark and the snow lay in heavy drifts, news came that once again we would have to be re-billeted. But this time all of us would have to leave the cottage. The owner now needed it for bombed out relations. It was very sad for our teachers who had made it their home and would now have to share with others. We awaited our fate with trepidation. The village was fuller than ever as bombing was intensified.

After about two weeks of searching, the billeting officer arrived one evening with news. We were banished to the kitchen to wash up while the situation was discussed.

"Make a noise with the dishes," Jean said, "while I listen at the keyhole." She overheard that the officer had pleaded our cause, saying we were the best behaved evacuees, and had eventually found us room at a farm cottage at Grange Farm. This was about two miles outside the village with a long dirt road leading to it. When we were called in from the kitchen we had to feign surprise at the news.

We were very familiar with the West Wratting road, it was one of our favourite directions, where we often took our picnics, but we had never been to the end of the track leading to the farm. This road was not cleared by the snowplough and my parents were contacted and asked to send us wellies. Once the decision was made, our move happened quickly. Our wellies had not arrived in time, the day was cold and bleak and the way was difficult as we trudged up the snow-covered drive with our few belongings. At the same time we felt excited, as long as we stayed together it would be another adventure.

Mr and Mrs Bacon were the nicest, kindest people we could ever expect to find and they had a daughter, Iris, who was between our ages, so we immediately became friends. An older daugher, Gwen, was in the land army and only home at weekends. Mr Bacon was not a young man and he worked very hard in the fields and looking after the farm animals.

Once again our diet completely changed. Nearly every day we had suet pudding, usually with meat inside. We loved it, as we were always desperately hungry, so nothing went to waste. Indeed, it must have been hard for Auntie Rene to feed us all. She made chocolate spread out of margarine, cocoa and a little sugar, which we adored. We picked dandelion leaves for our salads and there were always berries and apples in summer. The walk to school made us so hungry: two miles there and two miles back twice a day.

In summer we would sometimes take a short cut

Sunday Jan 19th. Iris Bacon drawn by Audrey Lanceman.

*Iris Bacon*
*drawn by*
*Audrey Lanceman*

through the cornfields, spurred on by the thought of suet pudding when we flagged at midday. Iris didn't go to the village school, she went to a secondary school in Cambridge and every day she would get the bus at the bottom of the drive. Each evening Jean and I would go down the road to meet her and we would march home singing the latest songs – usually those of Vera Lynn, Anne Shelton, The Ink Spots or Hutch's "It's a lovely day tomorrow" and other radio favourites. I was very fond of "The London I Love" or "London Pride", which we heard Noel Coward singing. The radio was our lifeline.

In the evenings, when a weary Mr Bacon came home from work, he would sink into his armchair next to the radio and listen to the news, followed by favourite comedy shows such as *ITMA* and *Much Binding in the Marsh*. There would be dance band music; Iris knew all the latest songs.

That first winter we were all gathered in the kitchen, each of us occupied in our own way, knitting, sewing, drawing, and Iris doing homework. The three cats would

*Mr Bacon*
*drawn by Audrey Lanceman*

come in from the barn and spread out with the dog before the fire. It was so cosy with the fire burning and the oil lamps lit. Then at bedtime we would take our small oil lamps up the stairs to the cold bedroom, which the three of us shared: Jean and me in the double bed and Iris in the single.

Mrs Bacon treated us all equally and never favoured Iris in front of us, indeed she told Iris off when we were really

*Mrs Bacon*
drawn by Audrey Lanceman

the guilty ones. We did a lot of dancing and jumping around before getting into bed with our stone hot-water bottle. On one occasion Jean was leaping about and crashed to the floor with a loud thump. Mrs Bacon called up the stairs, "Is that you, Iris, or a bomb?" knowing only too well it was Jean.

Even in winter we spent a lot of time out, if only to sit in the front porch with occasional forays into the barns or the plantation with the dog. She was a Scotch terrier called Vicki. We could play hide and seek in the barns, sometimes with the children from the neighbouring farm cottage. We didn't like them much as they caught moles and skinned them for their fur.

The coming of spring was such a delight on the farm, the snow slowly melting into rivulets and then into fast running brooks with the first snow drops pushing their way through the frozen earth, followed by violets and paigles.

Our walks to school were not so tedious as we sometimes took off our shoes and socks and paddled in the icy water in Clarke's meadow, which ran parallel to the road. This tree-lined meadow was one of our favourite places.

Carrying our gas masks everywhere was extremely irksome. We were always late for school after dinner but allowances were made. One day Squire Long, one of the few car owners in the village, stopped to give us a lift. He had never spoken to us before and we were rather in awe of him. We shyly got in but then he stopped twice to gossip with villagers. We dare not speak and by the time we got to school we were terribly late.

Auntie Rene had so much work to do with cooking and doing all the washing by hand that she asked us to carry back the week's shopping and rations on a Friday after school. We left our list with Mr Gedney on our way there and collected the shopping on the way back. We found it terribly heavy and took our time resting on the wayside every ten minutes and cursing our gas masks.

Iris was a wonderful friend and it was our constant singing with her that I remember most about her, as we walked through the woods and meadows. Our voices must have carried for miles.

Iris had grown up with the farm animals and each of them had a name. In the back meadow were three horses called Ginger, Jester and Judy. Early one frosty morning we were woken and told to come out and see the new foal that had just been born. We three rushed to the barn where the foal was struggling to its feet. The men tending the foal and its mother turned to us and said we could choose a name. "Winston" we all cried in unison.

We had never really been aware of the changing seasons in the city but in the country it was so interesting and exciting to see buds appear everywhere and then burst into the lush richness of summer. Corn and wheat ripened and tractors and ploughs were out till dusk, cutting and stacking the corn into sheaths. We children played hide and seek in the long grass and collected berries which Auntie Rene made into jams and pies.

I vividly recall a day, it was high summer, the three of us and the farm children next door had been playing at the end of a steep farm track. We were making our way back, the setting sun low in the sky, when suddenly there was the rumble of a farm wagon and coming down the hill at a pace was a wagon piled high with sugar beets, Uncle Eddie at the reins of a lumbering farm horse. It seemed to come down at an uncontrollable speed along the rutted track. We stood aside and I was struck by the beauty of the image before me, the rays of the sun silhouetting Mr Beeton and the great pile of beets, the great horse struggling with its precarious load. The sun's rays flecked with dust and hay particles behind him. I was unfamiliar with Constable but I could see the scene as a painting and that image is implanted in the eye of my memory forever.

Meanwhile the bombing continued in London. In their letters my mother told us that they were so weary of getting up nearly every night when there was a raid to go down to the shelter that they had made an arrangement with some friends who lived in London Colney. These friends no longer slept in their bed but slept in a Morrison shelter. They offered their bed to my parents, so every night after closing the shop my parents went out and crossed the road and got a lift from one of the many lorries that left London each evening. Each morning when they returned they never knew what to expect. And then one morning it happened, they arrived back in Holloway to devastation. The off-licence on the corner, a few doors away, had received a direct hit, our house was still standing but part of the roof over Jean's and my bedroom was

*Gwen – in the Land Army*
drawn by Audrey Lanceman

missing. The nice man in the off-licence, who used to save all the collection cards from his cigarette packets for us, was killed. As the house and shop were in an unstable condition and a mess my parents decided to pack up and go to Nottingham, where my mother had relatives, and search for somewhere to live.

I do not remember them visiting us at the Grange; they may have managed a visit before they moved to Nottingham. We had letters telling us of their difficulties but eventually my father found a shop to rent in the centre of the town. We digested the news as just one of those things, continued enjoying our life in the country but sang more sentimental songs about London. "The London I love" was a favourite.

Then quite suddenly it all came to an end. My parents wrote that they were coming to fetch us as we were now too far away for them to visit. They had found a billet for me, and one for David, in a village seven miles from Nottingham. Jean now having turned fourteen was to go out to work.

They came to fetch us the next Sunday in the car with balloons attached. I don't know why we felt so happy to be going home. There was hardly time to say goodbye to everyone. We didn't think about what lay ahead, we were going home. We left our dear friend Iris, our kind teachers and all our school friends, waving our way out of the village we also left our childhood behind.

## ✌ৡ *Chapter 3* ৡৡ

We didn't head straight for Nottingham. For some reason we went to London for a night. Perhaps my parents had things to see to or maybe they had not yet established themselves in Nottingham.

My familiar London was gone. As we drove through Islington there was so much bomb damage and an air of grey bleakness pervaded the streets. Arriving at our old house we saw that the end of the short terrace was shored up with wooden supports, at the other end was a crater where the landmine had exploded. My father took us for a walk round to see where the latest devastation had occurred. I remember half a house open to the elements, we saw into a bedroom, the wallpaper, the window frame, the remains of a bed. There were lots of people in the streets looking serious and purposeful as they scurried about. There was a noticeable lack of children.

Jean and I slept above the shop in my parents' bedroom; they must have slept in the workshop. I could not sleep, coming down from the quiet country I found London incredibly noisy. The trams thundered by every ten minutes, though there was a blackout there was a

*Collecting firewood. Islington Council had salvaged the joists and floorboards from bombed buildings and made the wood available for residents.*

reflected light travelling across the ceiling. On the ceiling centre there was a carved ceiling rose. I watched the light travel across it throughout most of the night and listened to voices and footsteps in the street and, for the first time, I wasn't so happy to have left that lovely village.

Next morning we drove off to Nottingham. The village we were taken to was not an attractive one. David and I were put in neighbouring council houses: me with a policeman's family, three boys and a girl. The middle boy was a bully and made my life miserable. Mrs P was harassed and overwhelmed by the difficulties of keeping house and feeding her flock. David next door was put with two girls. I don't know why I was not billeted there except that perhaps Mrs P. could not cope with another boy; her youngest was still a baby. Neither do I know why my parents thought her fit to look after me. Apparently my mother's cousins had known her when she was younger and in service and they therefore thought she was OK.

The house was ugly and utilitarian, with old lino in every room as I remember. Our diet was terrible, it consisted mainly of bread and dripping, so I assume we did have a Sunday roast. But I mainly remember being served tripe a lot, which I couldn't eat. There was a complete lack of fruit and veg. The combination of a dirty house and lack of vitamin C affected my health and I developed scabies, we all did and we were driven mad scratching. Elizabeth, the little girl I shared the bedroom with, was OK and quite good company but nothing like our friend Iris.

David was unhappy next door. The diet he had was equally peculiar. They had their pudding before their main course, one assumes in the hope that it would fill the children up. But David was quite happy at school, which I certainly wasn't. He had fared much better with his education at Balsham so that he could keep up. I was miles behind and had no idea how to answer my eleven-plus. What made matters worse was the sad fact that there were no art lessons at the village school, so that I could not shine in any way. My reaction to all this was to be very naughty and disruptive. During gas-mask drill, when we all had to sit for five minutes in our gas masks, I would blow rude noises through mine. The schoolmaster, an unsympathetic elderly Scotsman, got very exasperated with me and invariably I had to stay behind and write lines. I did have one or two friends who thought me amusing, I joined the Guides to be with them and to get out of the house but I was very unhappy.

Then my father made everything worse. He had never been religious, we were only half Jewish but he decided to forbid us to go to school during Jewish New Year. This was only a small village and there was nowhere for David and me to go. We just wandered about feeling like outcasts. After the holiday I experienced anti-Semitism for the first time. Dave, the nasty boy where I lived, became very spiteful. When his father left us sweets to share he would say, "Don't give her one. She's a Jew," and he would think up other spiteful acts to make my life miserable.

On Saturdays I would take the bus into Nottingham. The bus was usually full of shoppers heading for the market. My parents had a shop right in the centre of the town, backing onto the old lace market. The shop had an upstairs kitchen and living room, above that were two other rooms, not in very good shape especially the back room where my sister now slept, plaster missing from the ceiling, it was tiny and cramped, built in the early nineteenth century. Outside was a small, enclosed yard with the toilet housed in a dark outer shed. But to David and me it symbolised home and we longed to be there, and away from the village.

My parents however did not want to take any risks as there were still occasional raids, although other towns were now getting the worst of the bombing. The fact that there were the lace market factories to the rear, some of which had already been bombed, made their shop very vulnerable.

Jean, my sister, was equally unhappy. She was put into a succession of jobs, for which she had no training or liking. She worked her way through them, pretty fast – shop assistant, office girl, hairdresser's assistant – but her solace was to spend nearly every evening at Miss Anderson's School of Dancing, which eventually led her to a dancing part in the pantomime. This was at the Theatre Royal; the panto was Dick Whittington with George Formby.

The other reason we couldn't come home was lack of space. I also think my parents were having rather a nice time being right in the centre of town, opposite the George Hotel and in the vicinity of cinemas, pubs, clubs and the Palais de Dance. My mother also had several cousins in the area.

My father's shop was doing well and soon he opened another in the town. He had invented a short coat, called a box coat, which only required half the amount of clothing coupons needed for a long coat. They had brought their faithful machinist with them from London, she and my father worked at making these coats and selling them in the shop. They also began buying nice model coats from a wholesaler in London who my father went to school with. He was enjoying being a man about town, and would often nip off to the Palais de Dance for the tea dances. He was an excellent dancer; my mother was not keen partly because she had become quite deaf. The bombing had exacerbated what had been a minor problem.

I loved Saturdays in the town and felt deeply depressed having to take the bus back to the village at teatime. I don't remember how long I was there but I became less healthy, my head was itching all the time. Elizabeth and I did comb out fleas but nothing was done to eradicate them. When we all developed scabies nothing was done about that either and the itching was driving me mad. I scratched so much that I got infected sores on my back, which turned out to be impetigo. But I suppose what really made me unhappy was having no beauty or poetry in my life, nothing to nourish the soul or spirit. I still drew but almost secretly, no one was interested. David escaped from the reality by reading all the time, well into the night, but he had the advantage of doing well at school and earning the liking of the schoolmaster, which I didn't.

I remember pleading with my mother to take me home, but they could not see that there was much wrong with our billets as Mrs P was always very nice when they visited and they were also concerned about safety and their lack of space.

Things finally came to a head when one day I was scratching my head so much my mother decided to look into my hair and found it full of fleas and nits. She also looked at the awful sores on my back and took me straight to the doctor, who pronounced that I had impetigo and covered my wounds in a purple paint.

That was it. Much to our joy we were allowed to come home. How I recall our first night, David and me on makeshift mattresses side by side on the living room floor, as happy as larks. It was wonderful to be in the town. We saved our money and went every week to sit in the gods at the Empire Theatre to watch music hall and variety. There were some wonderful comedians and acts in those days, it was such a relief to laugh our heads off.

We all went to the cinema about twice a week, queuing for the cheap seats, it was sheer escapism watching those B movies with Bob Hope and Dorothy Lamour and romantic films with stars like Clark Gable, Hedy Lamarr, Betty Grable and dozens of others. One film in particular stuck in my memory, it was set on a desert island with lagoons, palm trees and Dorothy Lamour in a sarong. The male lead walked on screen and picked up a luscious fruit and sank his teeth into it, my mouth began to water, I was still vitamin C deprived and I longed for that fruit and could think of barely anything else for the remainder of the film.

It was fascinating being in the heart of Nottingham. From the window we could watch smart girls wander into the George Hotel across the road and then come out a little later arm in arm with officers. Trolley buses negotiated a sharp turn just by our windows and we were on eye-level with passengers when, as frequently happened, the arm came off the overhead wires and the conductor would drag out a long pole with a hook and reconnect the arm to the power line. On market days the centre would be swarming with people but at night it was usually quiet except for the sound of footsteps and people making their way home through the blackout. There was no traffic. I loved wandering in the lace market, there were interesting old alleys and cobbled streets and dramatic juxtapositions of bomb-damaged factories and bits of interesting architecture. It was specially nice at dusk when the area became quiet.

There were still air raids and when the siren went in the night we and the other cluster of resident shopkeepers left our beds and filed through the tobacconist's shop next door. At the back of the shop were stone steps leading down to the cellar, then a door and more steps, which were the entrance to the caves and one-time secret passage to the castle. It was cold but dry and safe. To pass the time until the all clear we found various activities, the grown ups would play cards or just talk but my sister took the opportunity to entertain us either with song or giving us the benefit of the dancing she had learned at Miss Anderson's dance classes. This greatly entertained our neighbours. There were no more big raids on Nottingham, other industrial towns were getting their turns but the darkest days of the blitz were over and our defences were stronger.

We had no facilities for bathing at home. We had to make do with a wash in the kitchen. So once or twice a week in the evening the whole family headed for the public washhouse. It was a wonderful old Victorian bathhouse. The baths were enormous and there were vast quantities of steaming hot water. It was jolly, stumbling home afterwards, arm in arm through the blackout.

David and I were sent to new schools, my girls' school, Sycamore Road, had very large classes. Once again I found myself way behind and in ignorance of things like maths. Nobody picked up on it and I was too shy to say anything. I usually sat at the back and my friends would tell me what to write, so I fumbled my way through lessons. We did have art classes though, and I could at last be good at something.

Our cramped housing spurred my father to do

something. We moved to a terraced house on the main Mansfield road. It was still rather dark and pokey and we still went to the public baths, but there was a little more space and we all acquired bicycles of various pedigrees. This enabled us to go out in the country on Sundays and on Thursdays' half-day closing. My mother had an aunt with a smallholding at Arnold. We loved going there as she kept chickens, ducks and bees. She also had fruit trees and bushes and we spent happy hours picking gooseberries and raspberries.

It was while we were at Mansfield Road that I heard about a junior art scholarship, which would get me into the College of Art at thirteen. I desperately wanted to go there and was so determined that I did not say anything to my parents in case they stopped me. They took it for granted that we girls did not need education; they did nothing to encourage our learning. Their attitude seemed to be that it wasn't for the likes of us, assuming we would either work in my father's shop or learn typing so that we could earn money until we got married.

Jean and I had other ideas, she was determined to be a dancer and I was equally determined to be an artist. I had trepidations about the exam as I lacked so much general education.

On the day I was to sit I set off alone and secretly, no one to wish me luck. I could not answer many of the general questions but made a good attempt, however when it came to the drawing side I had no problem and felt completely confident. By some miracle I was accepted.

The Nottingham College of Art was a lovely old building; it had a large life-drawing room and a sculpture room. There was a conservatory where plants were kept, which we could take away for our still life or nature drawing. It had a cast room where cast limbs and mouldings were kept. These were for the purposes of drawing as was the skeleton we drew to learn anatomy. In those days the accent was on learning to draw thoroughly, until we learned that we could not progress to painting. Understanding colour and tone and perspective were other priorities.

I suppose models were hard to get at that time for we had the same models for every session; a middle-aged Italian couple who took it in turns. I think we had two mornings of this. The class was always silent, there was no talking, except when the teacher left the room. The teaching method then was to give each of us a turn of instruction as the teacher worked his way round the room. Sometimes he looked over our shoulder and said, "Let me sit down," and he would proceed to do a thoroughly expert drawing on the margin to show us where we had gone wrong.

The sculpture room was more lively, we created heads or bodies on armature but the moment our teacher left the room we would pelt each other with pieces of clay. Our teacher would re-enter the class and in a weary voice say,

"Pick up the clay." There were several mature student Free Polish airmen who used the sculpture room. One Thursday afternoon one of them was missing. When the teacher enquired where he was someone told her, "He's gone to the Palais de Dance to study anatomy."

It was while we lived at Mansfield Road that the war began to draw to an end. The town was flooded with Americans; we watched endless convoys pass the house. In the evenings at around six or seven the skies became black with bombers. We stood in the street looking up, and waved and shouted "good luck" as the great noisy beasts filled the skies on their way to bomb the industrial towns of Germany.

The doodlebugs had begun in London and my cousin Betty came to live with us. She had been living in Stepney and now found, like many people, that the doodlebugs were the most frightening experience of the war, far worse than the blitz. She was a little younger than me and we had a lot of fun together, taking our bikes out to the country, and playing tennis. When the American convoys passed the house we rushed outside and stood at the curb so that we could get handouts of sweets and chewing gum. We scrambled with the other children to get the goodies as they were thrown.

The allies were advancing all over Europe after the D-day landings and the news was getting better each day. Then the glorious anticipated VE Day arrived: Victory in

Europe, Betty and I decided we had to be in London. Early next morning we rushed out of the house, crossed the road to get a bus to the station, but we couldn't wait for a bus, we thumbed a lorry and got a lift. Everyone was in buoyant mood.

We went to my uncle's house in St Albans. He had been bombed out of the East End. Accommodation was so scarce that nearly every room was let out to an odd assortment of lodgers. There was an old Romanian woman and her son Marcel, who was in the Free French Army. He was crazy about Paris and café chansons and he crooned all day. He taught us to sing "J'attendrais". There were two young women in another room, my uncle took them in and then found out one of them was pregnant, which was frowned on in those days. My grandmother also lived there, but there was always room for Betty and me, my uncle loved to have us there.

So that first victory May Day Uncle, Betty and I set off in the late afternoon for London in my uncle's old car. We were amongst the masses of revellers around Piccadilly, wedged in around Rainbow corner; we danced with half-drunk Americans and crazily happy cheering people.

We wanted to see the lights go on in Piccadilly after all those years of blackout so we sang "When the lights go on again all over the world". Meanwhile Americans were clambering up lamp posts with glasses of beer or hanging out of the windows of the Rainbow Club. After we had seen London lit up again and cheered ourselves hoarse we set off back to St Albans. It was quite late, the roads were empty and dark and our exhaust fell off creating a terrible din as we drove through quiet villages.

My cousin was still living with us when we moved again; it was the summer holidays and it was hot. This time we moved to a very nice semi-detached house in a leafy road in Sherwood. My father had managed to get a mortgage. The house was heaven and spacious and for the first time we had a bathroom, though I still shared a room with my sister, and never had my own room until she left home to attend the Rambert ballet school in Notting Hill. She managed to get a grant so that my father could not complain that he was supporting her, he had come to realise that she was not cut out to do mundane jobs.

It was at this house that the war with Japan ended and the six-year conflict was over. There was not quite the same euphoria as VE Day; the bombing of Hiroshima and Nagasaki was sobering and horrific. But the sigh of relief spread through the nation. Men were returning home to their families after years of separation and we could pick up the threads and return to normal life, even though life was grim with shortages and rationing until 1954. But at least there was hope and optimism that things would get better. For some children, things improved when they had their first taste of a banana.